MW00654957

PINTS *with* AQUINAS

50+ DEEP THOUGHTS *from*
THE ANGELIC DOCTOR

MATT FRADD

MacKillop Press

2016

Pints With Aquinas, 50+ Deep Thoughts From The Angelic Doctor

Matt Fradd

PUBLISHED BY MACKILLOP PRESS, ATLANTA GA

PRINTED IN THE UNITED STATES OF AMERICA

ISBN 978-0692752401

COVER AND BOOK DESIGN BY S.M. NELSON

TOTUS TUUS MARIA

ACKNOWLEDGMENTS

I would like to thank the following people who helped make this book possible. First I'd like to thank Fr Neil Dhabliwala who gave me his five volume set of the Summa Theologica a few years back. I've put it to good use! I'd also like to thank Steven Nelson (holynameholyface.com) for designing the inside and outside of this book. Thanks for being awesome, Steve. Finally I'd like to thank all of the listeners to my podcast, *Pints With Aquinas* (yep, in case you weren't aware, it's also a podcast). I deeply appreciate your support.

TABLE OF CONTENTS

Intro 7

God 11

Jesus 24

Grace 42

Sacraments 50

Virtue 63

Happiness 82

Alcohol 94

The Life of St. Thomas Aquinas 102

Podcast 120

Do you have a beer? You're going to need a beer.

IT'S OKAY.

I'LL WAIT.

If you could sit down with St. Thomas Aquinas over a pint of beer and ask him any one question, what would it be? In this book we'll ask him over 50 questions (don't worry, he's a patient guy) having to do with God, faith, virtue, the sacraments, and much else besides. You excited? You should be excited! In my experience there are three reasons people, who want to start reading Thomas Aquinas, feel too intimidated to do so. Here they are:

1. "UMM, IT'S ST. THOMAS! AS IN, 'I HAVE TO DICTATE UP TO FOUR SECRETARIES AT ONCE BECAUSE THAT'S HOW QUICK AND AWESOME

MY BRAIN IS.' THE DUDE'S REALLY SMART AND STUFF!"

Okay, so yeah, Aquinas is a really smart guy, obviously. He's probably the most respected theologian the Church has ever produced. That can be intimidating. But just because someone is intelligent and revered, doesn't mean they're impossible to understand. Aquinas actually writes quite simply and straightforwardly. As you'll discover, the man does not waste a word. What it takes modern theologians pages (or books) to say, he says in a couple of sentences. The excerpts I've chosen for this book are relatively short and uncomplicated. You'll be fine, I promise.

2. "HIS BOOKS ARE REALLY LONG AND HAVE NO PICTURES. I BARELY UNDERSTAND GREEN LANTERN COMICS AND THEY HAVE LOTS OF PICTURES."

Don't worry about the Green Lantern thing. I'm not sure Aquinas would have followed those either. It's true that Thomas writes voluminously (translation: a LOT), but that's okay, the Bible is big but you read that right? Right!?

Think of this book as a baby step. You don't have to read the entire Summa by next year, you'll get a lot just by reading the snippets contained in this book. It's my hope that this book will be a helpful introduction that might even inspire you to buy the Summa for yourself.

3. "HE USES WEIRD WORDS I DON'T UNDERSTAND. I DON'T LIKE NOT UNDERSTANDING THINGS. IT MAKES ME FEEL ANXIOUS, AND ANXIETY MAKES ME WANT TO EAT TOO MUCH ICE CREAM. I THINK ST. THOMAS IS WHY I'M OVERWEIGHT."

First, **#Whole30**. Second, it's true that St. Thomas uses metaphysical language that many modern readers have trouble understanding (motion, act, species, etc.), and so for the most part I've tried to only choose excerpts that don't contain a lot of those terms. If you would like a introduction to St. Thomas' metaphysical terms, listen to episode 18 of **Pints With Aquinas** entitled, *Understanding Thomas' Metaphysical Lingo*. You can learn more about the podcast on page 120. Let's get started.

GOD

1. IS THE EXISTENCE OF GOD SELF-EVIDENT?

A thing can be self-evident in either of two ways: on the one hand, self-evident in itself, though not to us; on the other, self-evident in itself, and to us. A proposition is self-evident because the predicate is included in the essence of the subject, as "Man is an animal," for animal is contained in the essence of man. If, therefore the essence of the predicate and subject be known to all, the proposition will be self-evident to all; as is clear with regard to the first principles of demonstration, the terms of which are common things that no one is ignorant of, such as being and non-being, whole and part, and such like.

If, however, there are some to whom the essence of the predicate and subject is unknown, the proposition will be self-evident in itself, but not to those who do not know the meaning of the predicate and subject of the proposition. Therefore, it happens, as Boethius says (Hebdom., the title of which is: "Whether all that is, is good"), "that there are some mental concepts self-evident only to the learned, as that incorporeal substances are not in space." Therefore I say that this proposition, "God exists," of itself is self-evident, for the predicate is the same as the subject, because God is His own [...]. Now because we do not know the essence of God, the proposition is not self-evident to us; but needs to be demonstrated by things that are more known to us, though less known in their nature—namely, by effects.

ST I, Q. 2, A. 1.

2. DOES GOD EXIST?

The first and more manifest way is the argument from motion. It is certain, and evident to our senses, that in the world some things are in motion. Now whatever is in motion is put in motion by another, for nothing can be in motion except it is in potentiality to that towards which it is in motion; whereas a thing moves inasmuch as it is in act. For motion is nothing else than the reduction of something from potentiality to actuality.

But nothing can be reduced from potentiality to actuality, except by something in a state of actuality. Thus that which is actually hot, as fire, makes wood, which is potentially hot, to be actually hot, and thereby moves and changes it. Now it is not possible that the same thing should be at once in actuality and potentiality in the same respect, but only in different respects. For what is actually hot cannot simultaneously be potentially hot; but it is simultaneously potentially cold. It is therefore impossible that in the same respect and in the same way a thing should be both mover and moved, i.e. that it should move itself.

Therefore, whatever is in motion must be put in motion by another. If that by which it is put in motion be itself put in motion, then this also must needs be put in motion by another, and that by another again. But this cannot go on to infinity, because then there would be no first mover, and, consequently, no other mover; seeing that subsequent movers move only inasmuch as they are put in motion by the first mover; as the staff moves only because it is put in motion by the hand. Therefore it is necessary to arrive at a first mover, put in motion by no other; and this everyone understands to be God.

ST I, Q. 2, A. 3.

3. IS GOD ALL GOOD?

To be good belongs pre-eminently to God. For a thing is good according to its desirableness. Now everything seeks after its own perfection; and the perfection and form of an effect consist in a certain likeness to the agent, since every agent makes its like; and hence the agent itself is desirable and has the nature of good. For the very thing which is desirable in it is the participation of its likeness. Therefore, since God is the first effective cause of all things, it is manifest that the aspect of good and of desirableness belong to Him; and hence Dionysius (Div. Nom. iv) attributes good to God as to the first efficient cause, saying that,

God is called good "as by Whom all things subsist."

ST I, Q. 6, A. 1.

4. IS GOD EVERYWHERE?

Since place is a thing, to be in place can be understood in a twofold sense; either by way of other things—i.e. as one thing is said to be in another no matter how; and thus the accidents of a place are in place; or by a way proper to place; and thus things placed are in a place. Now in both these senses, in some way God is in every place; and this is to be everywhere.

First, as He is in all things giving them being, power and operation; so He is in every place as giving it existence and locative power. Again, things placed are in place, inasmuch as they fill place; and God fills every place; not, indeed, like a body, for a body is said to fill place inasmuch as it excludes the co-presence of another body; whereas by God being in a place, others are not thereby excluded from it; indeed, by the very fact that He gives being to the things that fill every place, He Himself fills every place.

ST I, Q. 8, A. 2.

5. IS GOD ALL KNOWING?

In God there exists the most perfect knowledge. To prove this, we must note that intelligent beings are distinguished from non-intelligent beings in that the latter possess only their own form; whereas the intelligent being is naturally adapted to have also the form of some other thing; for the idea of the thing known is in the knower. Hence it is manifest that the nature of a non-intelligent being is more contracted and limited; whereas the nature of intelligent beings has a greater amplitude and extension; therefore the Philosopher says (De Anima iii) that "the soul is in a sense all things."

Now the contraction of the form comes from the matter. Hence, [...] forms according as they are the more immaterial, approach more nearly to a kind of infinity. Therefore it is clear that the immateriality of a thing is the reason why it is cognitive; and according to the mode of immateriality is the mode of knowledge. Hence it is said in De Anima ii that plants do not know, because they are wholly material. But sense is cognitive because it can receive images free from matter, and the intellect is still further cognitive, because it is more separated from matter and unmixed, as said in De Anima iii. Since therefore God is in the highest degree of immateriality [...], it follows that He occupies the highest place in knowledge.

ST I, Q. 14, A. 1.

6. IS GOD ALL POWERFUL?

All confess that God is omnipotent; but it seems difficult to explain in what His omnipotence precisely consists: for there may be doubt as to the precise meaning of the word 'all' when we say that God can do all things. If, however, we consider the matter aright, since power is said in reference to possible things, this phrase, "God can do all things," is rightly understood to mean that God can do all things that are possible; and for this reason He is said to be omnipotent. Now according to the Philosopher (Metaph. v, 17), a thing is said to be possible in two ways.

First in relation to some power, thus whatever is subject to human power is said to be possible to man. Secondly absolutely, on account of the relation in which the very terms stand to each other. Now God cannot be said to be omnipotent through being able to do all things that are possible to created nature; for the divine power extends farther than that. If, however, we were to say that God is omnipotent because He can do all things that are possible to His power, there would be a vicious circle in explaining the nature of His power. For this would be saying nothing else but that God is omnipotent, because He can do all that He is able to do.

It remains therefore, that God is called omnipotent because He can do all things that are possible absolutely; which is the second way of saying a thing is possible. For a thing is said to be possible or impossible absolutely, according to the relation in which the very terms stand to one another, possible if the predicate is not incompatible with the subject, as that Socrates sits; and absolutely impossible when the predicate is altogether incompatible with the subject, as, for instance, that a man is a donkey.

ST I, Q. 25, A. 3.

7. ARE ALL THINGS SUBJECT TO GOD'S PROVIDENCE?

Certain persons totally denied the existence of providence, as Democritus and the Epicureans, maintaining that the world was made by chance. Others taught that incorruptible things only were subject to providence and corruptible things not in their individual selves, but only according to their species; for in this respect they are incorruptible. They are represented as saying (Job 22:14): "The clouds are

His covert; and He doth not consider our things; and He walketh about the poles of heaven." Rabbi Moses, however, excluded men from the generality of things corruptible, on account of the excellence of the intellect which they possess, but in reference to all else that suffers corruption he adhered to the opinion of the others.

We must say, however, that all things are subject to divine providence, not only in general, but even in their own individual selves. This is made evident thus. For since every agent acts for an end, the ordering of effects towards that end extends as far as the causality of the first agent extends. Whence it happens that in the effects of an agent something takes place which has no reference towards the end, because the effect comes from a cause other than, and outside the intention of the agent. But the causality of God, Who is the first agent, extends to all being, not only as to constituent principles of species, but also as to the individualizing principles; not only of things incorruptible, but also of things corruptible. Hence all things that exist in whatsoever manner are necessarily directed by God towards some end; as the

Apostle says: "Those things that are of God are well ordered" (Romans 13:1).

Since, therefore, as the providence of God is nothing less than the type of the order of things towards an end, as we have said; it necessarily follows that all things, inasmuch as they participate in existence, must likewise be subject to divine providence. It has also been shown [...] that God knows all things, both universal and particular. And since His knowledge may be compared to the things themselves, as the knowledge of art to the objects of art, all things must of necessity come under His ordering; as all things wrought by art are subject to the ordering of that art.

ST I, Q. 22, A. 2.

8. CAN WE NAME GOD?

Since according to the Philosopher (Peri Herm. i), words are signs of ideas, and ideas the similitude of things, it is evident that words relate to the meaning of things signified through the medium of the intellectual conception. It follows therefore that we can give a name to anything in as far as we can understand it. Now [...], in this life we cannot see the essence of God; but we know God from creatures as their principle, and also by way of excellence and remotion. In this way therefore He can be named by us from creatures, yet not so that the name which signifies Him expresses the divine essence in itself. Thus the name "man" expresses the essence of man in himself, since it signifies the definition of man by manifesting his essence; for the idea expressed by the name is the definition. [...] The reason why God has no name, or is said to be above being named, is because His essence is above all that we understand about God, and signify in word.

ST I, Q. 13, A. 1.

9. WAS MARY A VIRGIN WHEN SHE CONCEIVED JESUS?

We must confess simply that the Mother of Christ was a virgin in conceiving for to deny this belongs to the heresy of the Ebionites and Cerinthus, who held Christ to be a mere man, and maintained that He was born of both sexes. It is fitting for four reasons that Christ should be born of a virgin. First, in order to maintain the dignity or the Father Who sent Him. For since Christ is the true and natural Son of God, it was not fitting that He should have another father than God: lest the dignity belonging to God be transferred to another.

Secondly, this was befitting to a property of the Son Himself, Who is sent. For He is the Word of God: and the word is conceived without any interior corruption: indeed, interior corruption is incompatible with perfect conception of the word. Since therefore flesh was so assumed by the Word of God, as to be the flesh of the Word of God, it was fitting that it also should be conceived without corruption of the mother.

Thirdly, this was befitting to the dignity of Christ's humanity in which there could be no sin, since by it the sin of the world was taken away, according to John 1:29: "Behold the Lamb of God" (i.e. the Lamb without stain) "who taketh away the sin of the world." Now it was not possible in a nature already corrupt, for flesh to be born from sexual intercourse without incurring the infection of original sin. Whence Augustine says (De Nup. et Concup. i): "In that union," viz. the marriage of Mary and Joseph, "the nuptial intercourse alone was lacking: because in sinful flesh this could not be without fleshly concupiscence which arises from sin, and without which He wished to be conceived, Who was to be without sin."

Fourthly, on account of the very end of Incarnation of Christ, which was that men might be born again as sons of God, "not of the will of the flesh, nor of the will of man, but of God" (John 1:13), i.e. of the power of God, of which fact the very conception of Christ was to appear as an exemplar. Whence Augustine says (De Sanct. Virg.): "It behooved that our Head, by a notable miracle, should be born, after the flesh, of a virgin, that He might thereby signify that His members would be born, after the Spirit, of a virgin Church."

ST III, Q. 28, A. 1.

10. WAS THE STAR THAT LEAD THE MAGI TO BETHLEHEM AN ACTUAL STAR?

As Chrysostom says (Hom. vi in Matth.), it is clear, for many reasons, that the star which appeared to the Magi did not belong to the heavenly system. First, because no other star approaches from the same quarter as this star, whose course was from north to south, these being the relative positions of Persia, whence the Magi came, and Judea.

Secondly, from the time [at which it was seen]. For it appeared not only at night, but also at midday: and no star can do this, not even the moon.

Grab a pint

ALE

Brewed with top fermenting yeast at cellar temperature, ales are fuller-bodied, with nuances of fruit or spice and a pleasantly hoppy finish. Generally robust and complex with a variety of fruit and malt aromas, ales come in many varieties. They could include Bitters, Milds, Abbey Ales, Pale Ales, Nut Browns, etc.

Ales are often darker than lagers, ranging from rich gold to reddish amber. Top fermenting, and more hops in the wort gives these beers a distinctive fruitfulness, acidity and pleasantly bitter seasoning. Ales have a more assertive, individual personality than lager, though their alcoholic strength is the same.

Thirdly, because it was visible at one time and hidden at another. For when they entered Jerusalem it hid itself: then, when they had left Herod, it showed itself again.

Fourthly, because its movement was not continuous, but when the Magi had to continue their journey the star moved on; when they had to stop the star stood still; as happened to the pillar of a cloud in the desert.

Fifthly, because it indicated the virginal Birth, not by remaining aloft, but by coming down below. For it is written (Matthew 2:9) that "the star which they had seen in the east went before them, until it came and stood over where the child was." Whence it is evident that the words of the Magi, "We have seen His star in the east," are to be taken as meaning, not that when they were in the east the star appeared over the country of Judea, but that when they saw the star it was in the east, and that it preceded them into Judea (although this is considered doubtful by some). But it could not have indicated the house distinctly, unless it were near the earth. And, as he [Chrysostom] observes, this does not seem fitting to a star, but "of some power endowed with reason." Consequently "it seems that this was some invisible force made visible under the form of a star."

Wherefore some say that, as the Holy Ghost, after our Lord's Baptism, came down on Him under the form of a dove, so did He appear to the Magi under the form of a star. While others say that the angel who, under a human form, appeared to the shepherds, under the form of a star, appeared to the Magi. But it seems more probable that it was a newly created star, not in the heavens, but in the air near the earth, and that its movement varied according to God's will. Wherefore Pope Leo says in a sermon on the Epiphany (xxxi): "A star of unusual brightness appeared to the three Magi in the east, which, through being more brilliant and more beautiful than the other stars, drew men's gaze and attention: so that they understood at once that such an unwonted event could not be devoid of purpose."

ST III, Q. 36, A. 7.

11. SHOULD WE GIVE THE SAME ADORATION TO CHRIST'S HUMANITY AS WE DO TO HIS GODHEAD?

We may consider two things in a person to whom honor is given: the person himself, and the cause of his being honored. Now properly speaking honor is given to a subsistent thing in its entirety: for we do not speak of honoring a man's hand, but the man himself. And if at any time it happen that we speak of honoring a man's hand or foot, it is not by reason of these members being honored of themselves: but by reason of the whole being honored in them. In this way a man may be honored even in something external; for instance in his vesture, his image, or his messenger. The cause of honor is that by reason of which the person honored has a certain excellence. for honor is reverence given to something on account of its excellence, [...].

If therefore in one man there are several causes of honor, for instance, rank, knowledge, and virtue, the honor given to him will be one in respect of the person honored, but several in respect of the causes of honor: for it is the man that is honored, both on account of knowledge and by reason of his virtue. Since, therefore, in Christ there is but one Person of the Divine and human natures, and one hypostasis, and one suppositum, He is given one adoration and one honor on the part of the Person adored: but on the part of the cause for which He is honored, we can say that there are several adorations, for instance that He receives one honor on account of His uncreated knowledge, and another on account of His created knowledge.

But if it be said that there are several persons or hypostases in Christ, it would follow that there would be, absolutely speaking, several adorations. And this is what is condemned in the Councils. For it is written in the chapters of Cyril [Council of Ephesus, Part I, ch. 26]: "If anyone dare to say that the man assumed should be adored besides the Divine Word, as though these were distinct persons; and does not rather honor the Emmanuel with one single adoration, inasmuch as the Word was made flesh; let him be anathema."

ST III, Q. 25, A. 1.

12. WAS IT FITTING THAT JESUS SHOULD BE TEMPTED?

Christ wished to be tempted; first that He might strengthen us against temptations. Hence Gregory says in a homily (xvi in Evang.): "It was not unworthy of our Redeemer to wish to be tempted, who came also to be slain; in order that by His temptations He might conquer our temptations, just as by His death He overcame our death."

Secondly, that we might be warned, so that none, however holy, may think himself safe or free from temptation. Wherefore also He wished to be tempted after His baptism, because, as Hilary says (Super Matth., cap. iii.): "The temptations of the devil assail those principally who are sanctified, for he desires, above all, to overcome the holy. Hence also it is written (Sirach 2): Son, when thou comest to the service of God, stand in justice and in fear, and prepare thy soul for temptation."

Thirdly, in order to give us an example: to teach us, to wit, how to overcome the temptations of the devil. Hence Augustine says (De Trin. iv) that Christ "allowed Himself to be tempted" by the devil, "that He might be our Mediator in overcoming temptations, not only by helping us, but also by giving us an example."

Fourthly, in order to fill us with confidence in His mercy. Hence it is written (Hebrews 4:15): "We have not a high-priest, who cannot have compassion on our infirmities, but one tempted in all things like as we are, without sin."

ST III, Q. 41, A. 1.

13. IN WHAT WAY IS CHRIST THE MEDIATOR OF GOD AND MAN?

Properly speaking, the office of a mediator is to join together and unite those between whom he mediates: for extremes are united in the mean [medio]. Now to unite men to God perfectively belongs to Christ, through Whom men are reconciled to God, according to 2 Corinthians 5:19: "God was in Christ reconciling the world to Himself." And, consequently, Christ alone is the perfect Mediator of God and men, inasmuch as, by His death, He reconciled the human race to God. Hence the Apostle, after saying, "Mediator of God and man, the man Christ Jesus," added: "Who gave Himself a redemption for all."

ST III, Q. 26, A. 1.

14. IS IT RIGHT TO SAY, "CHRIST AS MAN IS GOD"?

This term "man" when placed in the reduplication may be taken in two ways. First as referring to the nature; and in this way it is not true that Christ as Man is God, because the human nature is distinct from the Divine by a difference of nature. Secondly it may be taken as referring to the suppositum; and in this way, since the suppositum of the human nature in Christ is the Person of the Son of God, to Whom it essentially belongs to be God, it is true that Christ, as Man, is God. Nevertheless because the term placed in the reduplication signifies the nature rather than the suppositum, as stated above (Article 10), hence this is to be denied rather than granted: "Christ as Man is God."

ST III, Q. 16, A. 11.

15. WAS THE CRUCIFIXION OF CHRIST NECESSARY TO REDEEM MAN?

if [God] had willed to free man from sin without any satisfaction, He would not have acted against justice. For a judge, while preserving justice, cannot pardon fault without penalty, if he must visit fault committed against another—for instance, against another man, or against the State, or any Prince in higher authority.

But God has no one higher than Himself, for He is the sovereign and common good of the whole universe. Consequently, if He forgive sin, which has the formality of fault in that it is committed against Himself, He wrongs no one: just as anyone else, overlooking a personal trespass, without satisfaction, acts mercifully and not unjustly. And so David exclaimed when he sought mercy: "To Thee only have I sinned" (Psalm 50:6), as if to say: "Thou canst pardon me without injustice."

ST III, Q. 46, A. 2.

16. WAS IT NECESSARY THAT CHRIST SHOULD RISE FROM THE DEAD?

It behooved Christ to rise again, for five reasons. First of all; for the commendation of Divine Justice, to which it belongs to exalt them who humble themselves for God's sake, according to Luke 1:52: "He hath put down the mighty from their seat, and hath exalted the humble." Consequently, because Christ humbled

Himself even to the death of the Cross, from love and obedience to God, it behooved Him to be uplifted by God to a glorious resurrection; hence it is said in His Person (Psalm 138:2): "Thou hast known," i.e. approved, "my sitting down," i.e. My humiliation and Passion, "and my rising up," i.e. My glorification in the resurrection; as the gloss expounds.

Secondly, for our instruction in the faith, since our belief in Christ's Godhead is confirmed by His rising again, because, according to 2 Corinthians 13:4, "although He was crucified through weakness, yet He liveth by the power of God." And therefore it is written (1 Corinthians 15:14): "If Christ be not risen again, then is our preaching vain, and our faith is also vain": and (Psalm 29:10): "What profit is there in my blood?" that is, in the shedding of My blood, "while I go down," as by various degrees of evils, "into corruption?" As though He were to answer: "None. 'For if I do not at once rise again but My body be corrupted, I shall preach to no one, I shall gain no one,'" as the gloss expounds.

Thirdly, for the raising of our hope, since through seeing Christ, who is our head, rise again, we hope that we likewise shall rise again. Hence it is written (1 Corinthians 15:12): "Now if Christ be preached that He rose from the dead, how do some among you say, that there is no resurrection of the dead?" And (Job 19:25-27): "I know," that is with certainty of faith, "that my Redeemer," i.e. Christ, "liveth," having risen from the dead; "and" therefore "in the last day I shall rise out of the earth . . . this my hope is laid up in my bosom."

Fourthly, to set in order the lives of the faithful: according to Romans 6:4: "As Christ is risen from the dead by the glory of the Father, so we also may walk in newness of life": and further on; "Christ rising from the dead dieth now no more; so do you also reckon that you are dead to sin, but alive to God."

Fifthly, in order to complete the work of our salvation: because, just as for this reason did He endure evil things in dying that He might deliver us from evil, so was He glorified in rising again in order to advance us towards good things; according to Romans 4:25: "He was delivered up for our sins, and rose again for our justification."

ST III, Q. 53, A. 1.

GRACE

17. WHAT IS GRACE?

According to the common manner of speech, grace is usually taken in three ways. First, for anyone's love, as we are accustomed to say that the soldier is in the good graces of the king, i.e. the king looks on him with favor.

Secondly, it is taken for any gift freely bestowed, as we are accustomed to say: I do you this act of grace.

Thirdly, it is taken for the recompense of a gift given "gratis," inasmuch as we are said to be "grateful" for benefits. Of these three the second depends on the first, since one bestows something on another "gratis" from the love wherewith he receives him into his good "graces." And from the second proceeds the third, since from benefits bestowed "gratis" arises "gratitude." Now as regards the last two, it is clear that grace implies something in him who receives grace: first, the gift given gratis; secondly, the acknowledgment of the gift. But as regards the first, a difference must be noted between the grace of God and the grace of man; for since the creature's good springs from the Divine will, some good in the creature flows from God's love, whereby He wishes the good of the creature. On the other hand, the will of man is moved by the good pre-existing in things; and hence man's love does not wholly cause the good of the thing, but pre-supposes it either in part or wholly.

Therefore it is clear that every love of God is followed at some time by a good caused in the creature, but not co-eternal with the eternal love. And according to this difference of good the love of God to the creature is looked at differently. For one is common, whereby He loves "all things that are" (Wisdom 11:25), and thereby gives things their natural being. But the second is a special love, whereby He draws the rational creature above the condition of its nature to a participation of the Divine good; and according to this love He is said to love anyone simply, since it is by this love that God simply wishes the eternal good, which is Himself, for the creature. Accordingly when a man is said to have the grace of God, there is signified something bestowed on man by God. Nevertheless the grace of God sometimes signifies God's eternal love, as we say the grace of predestination, inasmuch as God gratuitously and not from merits predestines or or elects some; for it is written (Ephesians 1:5): "He hath predestinated us into the adoption of children . . . unto the praise of the glory of His grace."

ST I-II, Q. 110, A. 1.

18. CAN MAN BE SAVED WITHOUT THE GRACE OF GOD?

Acts conducing to an end must be proportioned to the end. But no act exceeds the proportion of its active principle; and hence we see in natural things, that nothing can by its operation bring about an effect which exceeds its active force, but only such as is proportionate to its power. Now everlasting life is an end exceeding the proportion of human nature [...]. Hence man, by his natural endowments, cannot produce meritorious works proportionate to everlasting life; and for this a higher force is needed, viz. the force of grace. And thus without grace man cannot merit everlasting life; yet he can perform works conducing to a good which is natural to man, as "to toil in the fields, to drink, to eat, or to have friends," and the like, as Augustine says in his third Reply to the Pelagians [Hypognosticon iii, among the spurious works of St. Augustine].

ST I-II, Q. 109, A. 5.

19. WHY IS THE JUSTIFICATION OF THE UNGODLY GOD'S GREATEST WORK?

A work may be called great in two ways: first, on the part of the mode of action, and thus the work of creation is the greatest work, wherein something is made from nothing; secondly, a work may be called great on account of what is made, and thus the justification of the ungodly, which terminates at the eternal good of a share in the Godhead, is greater than the creation of heaven and earth, which terminates at the good of mutable nature. Hence, Augustine, after saying that "for a just man to be made from a sinner is greater than to create heaven and earth," adds, "for heaven and earth shall pass away, but the justification of the ungodly shall endure."

ST I-II, Q. 113, A. 9.

Grab a pint

LAGER

Lager originates from the German word lagern which means 'to store' – it refers to the method of storing it for several months in near-freezing temperatures. Crisp and refreshing with a smooth finish from longer aging, lagers are the world's most popular beer (this includes pilseners).

A lager, which can range from sweet to bitter and pale to black, is usually used to describe bottom-fermented brews of Dutch, German, and Czech styles. Most, however, are a pale to medium color, have high carbonation, and a medium to high hop flavor.

SACRAMENTS

20. WHY ARE THERE SEVEN SACRAMENTS?

We may [...] gather the number of the sacraments from their being instituted as a remedy against the defect caused by sin. For Baptism is intended as a remedy against the absence of spiritual life; Confirmation, against the infirmity of soul found in those of recent birth; the Eucharist, against the soul's proneness to sin; Penance, against actual sin committed after baptism; Extreme Unction, against the remainders of sins--of those sins, namely, which are not sufficiently removed by Penance, whether through negligence or through ignorance; order, against divisions in the community; Matrimony, as a remedy against concupiscence in the individual, and against the decrease in numbers that results from death.

Some, again, gather the number of sacraments from a certain adaptation to the virtues and to the defects and penal effects resulting from sin. They say that Baptism corresponds to Faith, and is ordained as a remedy against original sin; Extreme Unction, to Hope, being ordained against venial sin; the Eucharist, to Charity, being ordained against the penal effect which is malice; order, to Prudence, being ordained against ignorance; Penance to Justice, being ordained against mortal sin; Matrimony, to Temperance, being ordained against concupiscence; Confirmation, to Fortitude, being ordained against infirmity.

ST III, Q. 65, A. 1.

21. IS IT OKAY TO BAPTIZE "IN THE NAME OF CHRIST"?

The sacraments derive their efficacy from Christ's institution. Consequently, if any of those things be omitted which Christ instituted in regard to a sacrament, it is invalid; save by special dispensation of Him Who did not bind His power to the sacraments. Now Christ commanded the sacrament of Baptism to be given with the invocation of the Trinity. And consequently whatever is lacking to the full invocation of the Trinity, destroys the integrity of Baptism. Nor does it matter that in the name of one Person another is implied, as the name of the Son is implied in that of theFather, or that he who mentions the name of only one Person may believe aright in the Three; because just as a sacrament requires sensible matter, so does it require a sensible form. Hence, for the validity of the sacrament it is not enough to imply or to believe in the Trinity, unless the Trinity be expressed in sensible words. For this reason at Christ's Baptism, wherein was the source of the sanctification of our Baptism, the Trinity was present in sensible signs: viz. the Father in the voice, the Son in the human nature, the Holy Ghost in the dove.

ST III, Q. 66, A. 6.

22. IN CONFESSION, DOES THE PRIEST HAVE TO PLACE HIS HANDS ON YOUR HEAD FOR IT TO BE VALID?

In the sacraments of the Church the imposition of hands is made, to signify some abundant effect of grace, through those on whom the hands are laid being, as it were, united to the ministers in whom grace should be plentiful. Wherefore an imposition of hands is made in the sacrament of Confirmation, wherein the fullness of the Holy Ghost is conferred; and in the sacrament of order, wherein is bestowed a certain excellence of power over the Divine mysteries; hence it is written (2 Timothy 1:6): "Stir up the grace of God which is in thee, by the imposition of my hands." Now the sacrament of Penance is ordained, not that man may receive some abundance of grace, but that his sins may be taken away; and therefore no imposition of hands is required for this sacrament, as neither is there for Baptism, wherein nevertheless a fuller remission of sins is bestowed.

ST III, Q. 84, A. 4.

23. CAN THE PRIEST EVER REVEAL WHAT HE HEARS IN CONFESSION?

The Decretal says (De Poenit. et Remiss., Cap. Omnis utriusque): "Let the priest beware lest he betray the sinner, by word, or sign, or in any other way whatever." Further, the priest should conform himself to God, Whose minister he is. But God does not reveal the sins which are made known to Him in confession, but hides them. Neither, therefore, should the priest reveal them. [...] Those things which are done outwardly in the sacraments are the signs of what takes place inwardly: wherefore confession, whereby a man subjects himself to a priest, a sign of the inward submission, whereby one submits to God. Now God hides the sins of those who submit to Him by Penance; wherefore this also should be signified in the sacrament of Penance, and consequently the sacrament demands that the confession should remain hidden, and he who divulges a confession sins by violating the sacrament. Besides this there are other advantages in this secrecy, because thereby men are more attracted to confession, and confess their sins with greater simplicity.

ST Suppl. Q. 11, A. 1.

24. IS THE EUCHARIST NECESSARY FOR SALVATION?

Two things have to be considered in this sacrament, namely, the sacrament itself, and what is contained in it. Now [...] the reality of the sacrament is the unity of the mystical body, without which there can be no salvation; for there is no entering into salvation outside the Church, just as in the time of the deluge there was none outside the Ark, which denotes the Church, according to 1 Peter 3:20-21. [...] [B]efore receiving a sacrament, the reality of the sacrament can be had through the very desire of receiving the sacrament. Accordingly, before actual reception of this sacrament, a man can obtain salvation through the desire of receiving it, just as he can before Baptism through the desire of Baptism [...]. Yet there is a difference in two respects. First of all, because

Baptism is the beginning of the spiritual life, and the door of the sacraments; whereas the Eucharist is, as it were, the consummation of the spiritual life, and the end of all the sacraments, [...] for by the hallowings of all the sacraments preparation is made for receiving or consecrating the Eucharist.

Consequently, the reception of Baptism is necessary for starting the spiritual life, while the receiving of the Eucharist is requisite for its consummation; by partaking not indeed actually, but in desire, as an end is possessed in desire and intention. Another difference is because by Baptism a man is ordained to the Eucharist, and therefore from the fact of children being baptized, they are destined by the Church to the Eucharist; and just as they believe through the Church's faith, so they desire the Eucharist through the Church's intention, and, as a result, receive its reality. But they are not disposed for Baptism by any previous sacrament, and consequently before receiving Baptism, in no way have they Baptism in desire; but adults alone have: consequently, they cannot have the reality of the sacrament without receiving the sacrament itself. Therefore this sacrament is not necessary for salvation in the same way as Baptism is.

ST III, Q. 73, A. 3.

25. DO YOU HAVE TO BE BAPTIZED BEFORE RECEIVING CONFIRMATION?

The character of Confirmation, of necessity supposes the baptismal character: so that, in effect, if one who is not baptized were to be confirmed, he would receive nothing, but would have to be confirmed again after receiving Baptism. The reason of this is that, Confirmation is to Baptism as growth to birth [...]. Now it is clear that no one can be brought to perfect age unless he be first born: and in like manner, unless a man be first baptized, he cannot receive the sacrament of Confirmation.

ST III, Q. 72, A. 6.

26. DOES MARRIAGE CONFER GRACE?

Matrimony, inasmuch as it is contracted in the faith of Christ, is able to confer the grace which enables us to do those works which are required in matrimony. and this is more probable, since wherever God gives the faculty to do a thing, He gives also the helps whereby man is enabled to make becoming use of that faculty; thus it is clear that to all the soul's powers there correspond bodily members by which they can proceed to act. Therefore, since in matrimony man receives by Divine institution the faculty to use his wife for the begetting of children, he also receives the the grace without which he cannot becomingly do so; just as we have said of the sacrament of orders [...]. And thus this grace which is given is the last thing contained in this sacrament.

ST Suppl. Q. 42, A. 3.

27. CAN A WOMAN BE ORDAINED?

Certain things are required in the recipient of a sacrament as being requisite for the validity of the sacrament, and if such things be lacking, one can receive neither the sacrament nor the reality of the sacrament. Other things, however, are required, not for the validity of the sacrament, but for its lawfulness, as being congruous to the sacrament; and without these one receives the sacrament, but not the reality of the sacrament. Accordingly we must say that the male sex is required for receiving Orders not only in the second, but also in the first way.

  Wherefore even though a woman were made the object of all that is done in conferring Orders, she would not receive Orders, for since a sacrament is a sign, not only the thing, but the signification of the thing, is required in all sacramental actions; thus [...] in Extreme Unction it is necessary to have a sick man, in order to signify the need of healing. Accordingly, since it is not possible in the female sex to signify eminence of degree, for a woman is in the state of subjection, it follows that she cannot receive the sacrament of

Order. Some, however, have asserted that the male sex is necessary for the lawfulness and not for the validity of the sacrament, because even in the Decretals (cap. Mulieres dist. 32; cap. Diaconissam, 27, qu. i) mention is made of deaconesses and priestesses. But deaconess there denotes a woman who shares in some act of a deacon, namely who reads the homilies in the Church; and priestess [presbytera] means a widow, for the word "presbyter" means elder.

ST Suppl. Q. 39, A. 1.

28. WAS ANOINTING OF THE SICK (EXTREME UNCTION) INSTITUTED BY CHRIST?

There are two opinions on this point. For some hold that this sacrament and Confirmation were not instituted by Christ Himself, but were left by Him to be instituted by the apostles; for the reason that these two sacraments, on account of the plenitude of grace conferred in them, could not be instituted before the mission of the Holy Ghost in perfect plenitude.

Hence they are sacraments of the New Law in such a way as not to be foreshadowed in the Old Law. But this argument is not very cogent, since, just as Christ, before His Passion, promised the mission of the Holy Ghost in His plenitude, so could He institute these sacraments. Wherefore others hold that Christ Himself instituted all the sacraments, but that He Himself published some, which present greater difficulty to our belief, while he reserved some to be published by the apostles, such as Extreme Unction and Confirmation. This opinion seems so much the more probable, as the sacraments belong to the foundation of the Law, wherefore their institution pertains to the lawgiver; besides, they derive their efficacy from their institution, which efficacy is given them by God alone.

ST Supple. Q. 29, A. 3.

VIRTUE

29. WHAT IS VIRTUE?

Virtue denotes a certain perfection of a power. Now a thing's perfection is considered chiefly in regard to its end. But the end of power is act. Wherefore power is said to be perfect, according as it is determinate to its act.

ST I-II, Q. 55, A. 1.

30. ARE THERE ONLY FOUR CARDINAL VIRTUES?

Things may be numbered either in respect of their formal principles, or according to the subjects in which they are: and either way we find that there are four cardinal virtues. For the formal principle of the virtue of which we speak now is good as defined by reason; which good is considered in two ways. First, as existing in the very act of reason: and thus we have one principal virtue, called "Prudence." Secondly, according as the reason puts its order into something else; either into operations, and then we have "Justice"; or into passions, and then we need two virtues. For the need of putting the order of reason into the passions is due to their thwarting reason: and this occurs in two ways. First, by the passions inciting to something against reason, and then the passions need a curb, which we call "Temperance." Secondly, by the passions withdrawing us from following the dictate of reason, e.g. through fear of danger or toil: and then man needs to be strengthened for that which reason dictates, lest he turn back; and to this end there is "Fortitude."

In like manner, we find the same number if we consider the subjects of virtue. For there are four subjects of the virtue we speak of now: viz. the power which is rational in its essence, and this is perfected by "Prudence"; and that which is rational by participation, and is threefold, the will, subject of "Justice," the concupiscible faculty, subject of "Temperance," and the irascible faculty, subject of "Fortitude."

ST I-II, Q. 61, A. 2.

Grab a pint

PORTER

Porter is a dark, almost black, fruity-dry, top fermenting style. An ale, porter is brewed with a combination of roasted malt to impart flavor, color and aroma. Stout is also a black, roast brew made by top fermentation.

31. IS FAITH A VIRTUE?

Since to believe is an act of the intellect assenting to the truth at the command of the will, two things are required that this act may be perfect: one of which is that the intellect should infallibly tend to its object, which is the true; while the other is that the will should be infallibly directed to the last end, on account of which it assents to the true: and both of these are to be found in the act of living faith. For it belongs to the very essence of faith that the intellect should ever tend to the true, since nothing false can be the object of faith, [...] while the effect of charity, which is the form of faith, is that the soul ever has its will directed to a good end. Therefore living faith is a virtue. On the other hand, lifeless faith is not a virtue, because, though the act of lifeless faith is duly perfect on the part of the intellect, it has not its due perfection as regards the will: just as if temperance be in the concupiscible, without prudence being in the rational part, temperance is not a virtue, [...] because the act of temperance requires both an act of reason, and an act of the concupiscible faculty, even as the act of faith requires an act of the will, and an act of the intellect.

ST II-II, Q. 4, A. 5.

32. IS FAITH INFUSED INTO MAN BY GOD?

Two things are requisite for faith. First, that the things which are of faith should be proposed to man: this is necessary in order that man believe anything explicitly. The second thing requisite for faith is the assent of the believer to the things which are proposed to him. Accordingly, as regards the first of these, faith must needs be from God. Because those things which are of faith surpass human reason, hence they do not come to man's knowledge, unless God reveal them. To some, indeed, they are revealed by God immediately, as those things which were revealed to the apostles and prophets, while to some they are proposed by God in sending preachers of the faith, according to Romans 10:15: "How shall they preach, unless they be sent?"

As regards the second, viz. man's assent to the things which are of faith, we may observe a twofold cause, one of external inducement, such as seeing a miracle, or being persuaded by someone to embrace the faith: neither of which is a sufficient cause, since of those who see the same miracle, or who hear the same sermon, some believe, and some do not. Hence we must assert another internal cause, which moves man inwardly to assent to matters of faith. The Pelagians held that this cause was nothing else than man's free-will: and consequently they said that the beginning of faith is from ourselves, inasmuch as, to wit, it is in our power to be ready to assent to things which are of faith, but that the consummation of faith is from God, Who proposes to us the things we have to believe. But this is false, for, since man, by assenting to matters of faith, is raised above his nature, this must needs accrue to him from some supernatural principle moving him inwardly; and this is God. Therefore faith, as regards the assent which is the chief act of faith, is from God moving man inwardly by grace.

ST II-II, Q. 6, A. 1.

33. DO THE DEMONS HAVE FAITH?

[T]he believer's intellect assents to that which he believes, not because he sees it either in itself, or by resolving it to first self-evident principles, but because his will commands his intellect to assent. Now, that the will moves the intellect to assent, may be due to two causes. First, through the will being directed to the good, and in this way, to believe is a praiseworthy action.

Secondly, because the intellect is convinced that it ought to believe what is said, though that conviction is not based on objective evidence. Thus if a prophet, while preaching the word of God, were to foretell something, and were to give a sign, by raising a dead person to life, the intellect of a witness would be convinced so as to recognize clearly that God, Who lieth not, was speaking, although the thing itself foretold would not be evident in itself, and consequently the essence of faith would not be removed. Accordingly we must say that faith is commended in the first sense in the faithful of Christ: and in this way faith is not in the demons, but only in the second way, for they see many evident signs, whereby they recognize that the teaching of the Church is from God, although they do not see the things themselves that the Church teaches, for instance that there are three Persons in God, and so forth.

ST II-II, Q. 5, A. 2.

34. IS HOPE A VIRTUE?

According to the Philosopher (Ethic. ii, 6) "the virtue of a thing is that which makes its subject good, and its work good likewise." Consequently wherever we find a good human act, it must correspond to some human virtue. Now in all things measured and ruled, the good is that which attains its proper rule: thus we say that a coat is good if it neither exceeds nor falls short of its proper measurement. But [...] human acts have a twofold measure; one is proximate and homogeneous, viz. the reason, while the other is remote and excelling, viz. God: wherefore every human act is good, which attains reason or God Himself. Now the act of hope, whereof we speak now, attains God. For, [...] when we were treating of the passion of hope, the object of hope is a future good, difficult but possible to obtain. Now a thing is possible to us in two ways: first, by ourselves; secondly, by means of others, as stated in Ethic. iii. Wherefore, in so far as we hope for anything as being possible to us by means of the Divine assistance, our hope attains God Himself, on Whose help it leans. It is therefore evident that hope is a virtue, since it causes a human act to be good and to attain its due rule.

ST II-II, Q. 17, A. 1.

35. IS CHARITY A VIRTUE?

Augustine says (De Moribus Eccl. xi): "Charity is a virtue which, when our affections are perfectly ordered, unites us to God, for by it we love Him." [...] Human acts are good according as they are regulated by their due rule and measure. Wherefore human virtue which is the principle of all man's good acts consists in following the rule of human acts, which is twofold, [...] human reason and God. Consequently just as moral virtue is defined as being "in accord with right reason," as stated in Ethic. ii, 6, so too, the nature of virtue consists in attaining God [...]. Wherefore, it follows that charity is a virtue, for, since charity attains God, it unites us to God, as evidenced by the authority of Augustine quoted above.

ST II-II, Q. 23, A. 3.

36. SHOULD WE LOVE THE DEMONS OUT OF CHARITY?

In the sinner, we are bound, out of charity, to love his nature, but to hate his sin. But the name of demon is given to designate a nature deformed by sin, wherefore demons should not be loved out of charity. Without however laying stress on the word, the question as to whether the spirits called demons ought to be loved out of charity, must be answered [by recognizing] that a thing may be loved out of charity in two ways. First, a thing may be loved as the person who is the object of friendship, and thus we cannot have the friendship of charity towards the demons. For it is an essential part of friendship that one should be a well-wisher towards one's friend; and it is impossible for us, out of charity, to desire the good of everlasting life, to which charity is referred, for those spirits whom God has condemned eternally, since this would be in opposition to our charity towards God whereby we approve of His justice.

Secondly, we love a thing as being that which we desire to be enduring as another's good. On this way we love irrational creatures out of charity, in as much as we wish them to endure, to give glory to God and be useful to man, [...] and in this way too we can love the nature of the demons even out of charity, in as much as we desire those spirits to endure,

as to their natural gifts, unto God's glory.

ST II-II, Q. 25, A. 11.

37. IS PRUDENCE A VIRTUE?

[G]ood may be understood in a twofold sense: first, materially, for the thing that is good, secondly, formally, under the aspect of good. Good, under the aspect of good, is the object of the appetitive power. Hence if any habits rectify the consideration of reason, without regarding the rectitude of the appetite, they have less of the nature of a virtue since they direct man to good materially, that is to say, to the thing which is good, but without considering it under the aspect of good. On the other hand those virtues which regard the rectitude of the appetite, have more of the nature of virtue, because they consider the good not only materially, but also formally, in other words, they consider that which is good under the aspect of good. Now it belongs to prudence [...] to apply right reason to action, and this is not done without aright appetite. Hence prudence has the nature of virtue not only as the other intellectual virtues have it, but also as the moral virtues have it, among which virtues it is enumerated.

ST II-II, Q. 47, A. 4.

38. IS JUSTICE A VIRTUE?

A human virtue is one "which renders a human act and man himself good" [Ethic. ii, 6, and this can be applied to justice. For a man's act is made good through attaining the rule of reason, which is the rule whereby human acts are regulated. Hence, since justice regulates human operations, it is evident that it renders man's operations good, and, as Tully declares (De Officiis i, 7), good men are so called chiefly from their justice, wherefore, as he says again (De Officiis i, 7) "the luster of virtue appears above all in justice."

ST II-II, Q. 58, A. 3.

39. IS FORTITUDE A VIRTUE?

Human virtue, of which we are speaking now, is that which makes a man good, and tenders his work good. Now man's good is to be in accordance with reason, according to Dionysius (Div. Nom. iv, 22). Wherefore it belongs to human virtue to make man good, to make his work accord with reason. This happens in three ways: first, by rectifying reason itself, and this is done by the intellectual virtues; secondly, by establishing the rectitude of reason in human affairs, and this belongs to justice; thirdly, by removing the obstacles to the establishment of this rectitude inhuman affairs. Now the human will is hindered in two ways from following the rectitude of reason. First, through being drawn by some object of pleasure to something other than what the rectitude of reason requires; and this obstacle is removed by the virtue of temperance. Secondly, through the will being disinclined to follow that which is in accordance with reason, on account of some difficulty that presents itself. On order to remove this obstacle fortitude of the mind is requisite, whereby to resist the aforesaid difficulty even as a man, by fortitude of body, overcomes and removes bodily obstacles.

ST II-II, Q. 123, A. 1.

40. IS TEMPERANCE A VIRTUE?

It is essential to virtue to incline man to good. Now the good of man is to be in accordance with reason, as Dionysius states (Div. Nom. iv). Hence human virtue is that which inclines man to something in accordance with reason. Now temperance evidently inclines man to this, since its very name implies moderation or temperateness, which reason causes. Therefore temperance is a virtue.

ST II-II, Q. 141, A. 1.

Grab a pint

STOUT

There's very little distinction between a Stout and a Porter, but they do have their differences. Stout, not as sweet to the taste, features a rich, creamy head and is flavored and colored by barley. Stouts often use a portion of unmalted roasted barley to develop a dark, slightly astringent, coffee-like character.

41. IS IT POSSIBLE TO BE HAPPY?

Happiness is the attainment of the Perfect Good.
Whoever, therefore, is capable of the Perfect Good
can attain Happiness. Now, that man is capable of
the Perfect Good, is proved both because his intellect
can apprehend the universal and perfect good, and
because his will can desire it. And therefore man can
attain Happiness. This can be proved again from the
fact that man is capable of seeing God, [...] in which
vision, [...] man's perfect Happiness consists.

ST I-II, Q. 5, A. 1.

42. IS IT POSSIBLE TO BE HAPPY IN THIS LIFE?

Since happiness is a "perfect and sufficient good," it
excludes every evil, and fulfils every desire. But in this
life every evil cannot be excluded. For this present
life is subject to many unavoidable evils; to ignorance
on the part of the intellect; to inordinate affection on
the part of the appetite, and to many penalties on the

part of the body; as Augustine sets forth in De Civ. Dei xix, 4. Likewise neither can the desire for good be satiated in this life. For man naturally desires the good, which he has, to be abiding. Now the goods of the present life pass away; since life itself passes away, which we naturally desire to have, and would wish to hold abidingly, for man naturally shrinks from death. Wherefore it is impossible to have true Happiness in this life.

ST I-II, Q. 5, A. 3.

43. WILL MONEY MAKE ME HAPPY?

It is impossible for man's happiness to consist in wealth. For wealth is twofold, as the Philosopher says (Polit. i, 3), viz. natural and artificial. Natural wealth is that which serves man as a remedy for his natural wants: such as food, drink, clothing, cars, dwellings, and such like, while artificial wealth is that which is not a direct help to nature, as money, but is invented by the art of man, for the convenience of exchange, and as a measure of things salable. Now it is evident that man's happiness cannot consist in natural wealth. For wealth of this kind is sought for the sake of something else, viz. as a support of human nature: consequently it cannot be man's last end, rather is it ordained to man as to its end. Wherefore in the order of nature, all such things are below man, and made for him, according to Psalm 8:8: "Thou hast subjected all things under his feet." And as to artificial wealth, it is not sought save for the sake of natural wealth; since man would not seek it except because, by its means, he procures for himself the necessaries of life. Consequently much less can it be considered in the light of the last end. Therefore it is impossible for happiness, which is the last end of man, to consist in wealth.

ST I-II, Q. 2, A. 1.

44. WILL THE RESPECT OF OTHERS MAKE ME HAPPY?

It is impossible for happiness to consist in honor. For honor is given to a man on account of some excellence in him; and consequently it is a sign and attestation of the excellence that is in the person honored. Now a man's excellence is in proportion, especially to his happiness, which is man's perfect good; and to its parts, i.e. those goods by which he has a certain share of happiness. And therefore honor can result from happiness, but happiness cannot principally consist therein.

ST I-II, Q. 2, A. 2.

45. WILL BEING FAMOUS MAKE ME HAPPY?

Man's happiness cannot consist in human fame or glory. For glory consists "in being well known and praised," as Ambrose [Augustine, Contra Maxim. Arian. ii, 13] says. Now the thing known is related to human knowledge otherwise than to God's knowledge: for human knowledge is caused by the things known, whereas God's knowledge is the cause of the things known. Wherefore the perfection of human good, which is called happiness, cannot be caused by human knowledge: but rather human knowledge of another's happiness proceeds from, and, in a fashion, is caused by, human happiness itself, inchoate or perfect. Consequently man's happiness cannot consist in fame or glory.

ST I-II, Q. 2, A. 3.

46. WILL BEING POWERFUL MAKE ME HAPPY?

It is impossible for happiness to consist in power; and this for two reasons. First because power has the nature of principle, as is stated in Metaph. v, 12, whereas happiness has the nature of last end. Secondly, because power has relation to good and evil: whereas happiness is man's proper and perfect good. Wherefore some happiness might consist in the good use of power, which is by virtue, rather than in power itself. Now four general reasons may be given to prove that happiness consists in none of the foregoing external goods. First, because, since happiness is man's supreme good, it is incompatible with any evil. Now all the foregoing can be found both in good and in evil men.

Secondly, because, since it is the nature of happiness to "satisfy of itself," as stated in Ethic. i, 7, having gained happiness, man cannot lack any needful good. But after acquiring any one of the foregoing, man may still lack many goods that are necessary to him; for instance, wisdom, bodily health, and such like.

Thirdly, because, since happiness is the perfect good, no evil can accrue to anyone therefrom. This cannot be said of the foregoing: for it is written (Ecclesiastes 5:12) that "riches" are sometimes "kept to the hurt of the owner"; and the same may be said of the other three.

Fourthly, because man is ordained to happiness

through principles that are in him; since he is ordained thereto naturally. Now the four goods mentioned above are due rather to external causes, and in most cases to fortune; for which reason they are called goods of fortune. Therefore it is evident that happiness nowise consists in the foregoing.

ST I-II, Q. 2, A. 4.

47. WILL PLEASURE MAKE ME HAPPY?

Because bodily delights are more generally known, "the name of pleasure has been appropriated to them" (Ethic. vii, 13), although other delights excel them: and yet happiness does not consist in them. Because in every thing, that which pertains to its essence is distinct from its proper accident: thus in man it is one thing that he is a mortal rational animal, and another that he is a risible animal. We must therefore consider that every delight is a proper accident resulting from happiness, or from some part of happiness; since the reason that a man is delighted is that he has some fitting good, either in reality, or in hope, or at least in memory. Now a fitting good, if indeed it be the perfect good, is precisely man's happiness: and if it is imperfect, it is a share of happiness, either proximate, or remote, or at least apparent. Therefore it is evident that neither is delight, which results from the perfect good, the very essence of happiness, but something resulting therefrom as its proper accident.

But bodily pleasure cannot result from the perfect good even in that way. For it results from a good apprehended by sense, which is a power of the soul, which power makes use of the body. Now good pertaining to the body, and apprehended by sense, cannot be man's perfect good. For since the rational soul excels the capacity of corporeal matter, that part of the soul which is independent of a corporeal organ, has a certain infinity in regard to the body and those parts of the soul which are tied down to the body: just as immaterial things are in a way infinite as compared to material things, since a form is, after a fashion, contracted and bounded by matter, so that a form which is independent of matter is, in a way, infinite.

Therefore sense, which is a power of the body, knows the singular, which is determinate through matter: whereas the intellect, which is a power independent of matter, knows the universal, which is abstracted from matter, and contains an infinite number of singulars. Consequently it is evident that good which is fitting to the body, and which causes bodily delight through being apprehended by sense, is not man's perfect good, but is quite a trifle as compared with the good of the soul. Hence it is written (Wisdom 7:9) that "all gold in comparison of her, is as a little sand." And therefore bodily pleasure is neither happiness itself, nor a proper accident of happiness.

ST I-II, Q. 2, A. 6.

48. WHAT THEN WILL MAKE ME HAPPY?

Final and perfect happiness can consist in nothing else than the vision of the Divine Essence. To make this clear, two points must be observed. First, that man is not perfectly happy, so long as something remains for him to desire and seek: secondly, that the perfection of any power is determined by the nature of its object. Now the object of the intellect is "what a thing is," i.e. the essence of a thing, according to De Anima iii, 6. Wherefore the intellect attains perfection, in so far as it knows the essence of a thing. If therefore an intellect knows the essence of some effect, whereby it is not possible to know the essence of the cause, i.e. to know of the cause "what it is"; that intellect cannot be said to reach that cause simply, although it may be able to gather from the effect the knowledge of that the cause is.

Consequently, when man knows an effect, and knows that it has a cause, there naturally remains in the man the desire to know about the cause, "what it is." And this desire is one of wonder, and causes inquiry, as is stated in the beginning of the Metaphysics (i, 2). For instance, if a man, knowing the eclipse of the sun, consider that it must be due to some cause, and know not what that cause is, he wonders about it, and from wondering proceeds to inquire. Nor does this inquiry cease until he arrive at a knowledge of the essence of the cause. If therefore the human intellect, knowing

Happiness

the essence of some created effect, knows no more of God than "that He is"; the perfection of that intellect does not yet reach simply the First Cause, but there remains in it the natural desire to seek the cause. Wherefore it is not yet perfectly happy. Consequently, for perfect happiness the intellect needs to reach the very Essence of the First Cause. And thus it will have its perfection through union with God as with that object, in which alone man's happiness consists.

ST I-II, Q. 3, A. 8.

Page 93

ALCOHOL

49. IS IT WRONG TO DRINK ALCOHOL?

No meat or drink, considered in itself, is unlawful, according to Matthew 15:11, "Not that which goeth into the mouth defileth a man." Wherefore it is not unlawful to drink wine as such. Yet it may become unlawful accidentally. This is sometimes owing to a circumstance on the part of the drinker, either because he is easily the worse for taking wine, or because he is bound by a vow not to drink wine: sometimes it results from the mode of drinking, because to wit he exceeds the measure in drinking: and sometimes it is on account of others who would be scandalized thereby.

ST II-II, Q. 149, A. 3.

50. IS IT A MORTAL SIN TO GET DRUNK?

The sin of drunkenness [...] consists in the immoderate use and concupiscence of wine. Now this may happen to a man in three ways. First, so that he knows not the drink to be immoderate and intoxicating: and then drunkenness may be without sin [...].

Secondly, so that he perceives the drink to be immoderate, but without knowing it to be intoxicating, and then drunkenness may involve a venial sin.

Thirdly, it may happen that a man is well aware that the drink is immoderate and intoxicating, and yet he would rather be drunk than abstain from drink. Such a man is a drunkard properly speaking, because morals take their species not from things that occur accidentally and beside the intention, but from that which is directly intended. On this way drunkenness is a mortal sin, because then a man willingly and knowingly deprives himself of the use of reason, whereby he performs virtuous deeds and avoids sin, and thus he sins mortally by running the risk of falling into sin. For Ambrose says (De Patriarch. [De Abraham i.]): "We learn that we should shun drunkenness, which prevents us from avoiding grievous sins. For the things we avoid when sober, we unknowingly commit through drunkenness." Therefore drunkenness, properly speaking, is a mortal sin.

ST II-II, Q. 150, A. 2.

51. IS ONE GUILTY OF THE SINS HE COMMITS WHILE DRUNK?

According to Augustine (Contra Faust. xxii, 43), Lot was to be excused from incest on account of drunkenness. [. . .] Two things are to be observed in drunkenness, [...] namely the resulting defect and the preceding act. on the part of the resulting defect whereby the use of reason is fettered, drunkenness may be an excuse for sin, in so far as it causes an act to be involuntary through ignorance. But on the part of the preceding act, a distinction would seem necessary; because, if the drunkenness that results from that act be without sin, the subsequent sin is entirely excused from fault, as perhaps in the case of Lot. If, however, the preceding act was sinful, the person is not altogether excused from the subsequent sin, because the latter is rendered voluntary through the voluntariness of the preceding act, inasmuch as it was through doing something unlawful that he fell into the subsequent sin. Nevertheless, the resulting sin is diminished, even as the character of voluntariness is diminished. Wherefore Augustine says (Contra Faust. xxii, 44) that "Lot's guilt is to be measured, not by the incest, but by his drunkenness."

ST II-II, Q. 150, A. 4.

Grab a pint

MALT

Generally dark and sweeter in flavor, malts contain hints of caramel, toffee, and nuts. They can be light to full bodied.

THE LIFE OF ST. THOMAS AQUINAS

The great outlines and all the important events of his life are known, but biographers differ as to some details and dates. Death prevented Henry Denifle from executing his project of writing a critical life of the saint. Denifle's friend and pupil, Dominic Prümmer, O.P., professor of theology in the University of Fribourg, Switzerland, took up the work and published the "Fontes Vitae S. Thomae Aquinatis, notis historicis et criticis illustrati"; and the first fascicle (Toulouse, 1911) has appeared, giving the life of St. Thomas by Peter Calo (1300) now published for the first time. From Tolomeo of Lucca . . . we learn that at the time of the saint's death there was a doubt about his exact age (Prümmer, op. cit., 45). The end of 1225 is usually assigned as the time of his birth. Father Prümmer, on the authority of Calo, thinks 1227 is the more probable date (op. cit., 28). All agree that he died in 1274.

Landulph, his father, was Count of Aquino; Theodora, his mother, Countess of Teano. His family was related to the Emperors Henry VI and Frederick II, and to the Kings of Aragon, Castile, and France. Calo relates that a holy hermit foretold his career, saying to Theodora before his birth: "He will enter the Order of Friars Preachers, and so great will be his learning and sanctity that in his day no one will be found to equal him" (Prümmer, op. cit., 18). At the age of five, according to the custom of the times, he was sent to receive his first training from the Benedictine monks of Monte Cassino. Diligent in study, he was thus early noted as being meditative and devoted to prayer, and his preceptor was surprised at hearing the child ask frequently: "What is God?"

About the year 1236 he was sent to the University of Naples. Calo says that the change was made at the instance of the Abbot of Monte Cassino, who wrote to Thomas's father that a boy of such talents should not be left in obscurity (Prümmcr, op. cit., 20). At Naples his prcceptors were Pietro Martini and Petrus Hibernus. The chronicler says that he soon surpassed Martini at grammar, and he was then given over to Peter of Ireland, who trained him in logic and the natural sciences. The customs of the times divided the liberal arts into two courses: the Trivium, embracing grammar, logic, and rhetoric; the Quadrivium, comprising music, mathematics, geometry, and astronomy . . . . Thomas could repeat the lessons with more depth and lucidity than his masters displayed. The youth's heart had remained pure amidst the corruption with which he was surrounded, and he resolved to embrace the religious life.

Some time between 1240 and August, 1243, he received the habit of the Order of St. Dominic, being attracted and directed by John of St. Julian, a noted preacher of the convent of Naples. The city wondered that such a noble young man should don the garb of poor friar. His mother, with mingled feelings of joy and sorrow, hastened to Naples to see her son. The Dominicans, fearing she would take him away, sent him to Rome, his ultimate destination being Paris or Cologne. At the instance of Theodora, Thomas's brothers, who were soldiers under the Emperor Frederick, captured the novice near the town of Aquapendente and confined him in the fortress of San Giovanni at Rocca Secca. Here he was detained nearly two years, his parents, brothers, and sisters endeavouring by various means to destroy his vocation. The brothers even laid snares for his virtue, but the pure-minded novice drove the temptress from his room with a brand which he snatched from the fire. Towards the end of his life, St. Thomas confided to his faithful friend and companion, Reginald of Piperno, the secret of a remarkable favour received at this time. When the temptress had been driven from his chamber, he knelt and most earnestly implored God to grant him integrity of mind and body. He fell into a gentle sleep, and, as he slept, two angels appeared to assure him that his prayer had been heard. They then girded him about with a white girdle, saying: "We gird thee with the girdle of perpetual virginity." And from that day forward he never experienced the slightest motions of concupiscence.

The time spent in captivity was not lost. His mother relented somewhat, after the first burst of anger and grief; the Dominicans were allowed to provide him with new habits, and through the kind offices of his sister he procured some books — the Holy Scriptures, Aristotle's Metaphysics, and the "Sentences" of Peter

Lombard. After eighteen months or two years spent in prison, either because his mother saw that the hermit's prophecy would eventually be fulfilled or because his brothers feared the threats of Innocent IV and Frederick II, he was set at liberty, being lowered in a basket into the arms of the Dominicans, who were delighted to find that during his captivity "he had made as much progress as if he had been in a studium generale" (Calo, op. cit., 24).

Thomas immediately pronounced his vows, and his superiors sent him to Rome. Innocent IV examined closely into his motives in joining the Friars Preachers, dismissed him with a blessing, and forbade any further interference with his vocation. John the Teutonic, fourth master general of the order, took the young student to Paris and, according to the majority of the saint's biographers, to Cologne, where he arrived in 1244 or 1245, and was placed under Albertus Magnus, the most renowned professor of the order. In the schools Thomas's humility and taciturnity were misinterpreted as signs of dullness, but when Albert had heard his brilliant defence of a difficult thesis, he exclaimed: "We call this young man a dumb ox, but his bellowing in doctrine will one day resound throughout the world."

In 1245 Albert was sent to Paris, and Thomas accompanied him as a student. In 1248 both returned to Cologne. Albert had been appointed regent of the new studium generale, erected that year by the general chapter of the order, and Thomas was to teach under him as Bachelor. (On the system of graduation in the thirteenth century see ORDER OF PREACHERS — II, A, 1, d). During his stay in Cologne, probably in 1250, he was raised to the priesthood by Conrad of Hochstaden, archbishop of that city. Throughout his busy life, he frequently preached the Word of God, in Germany, France, and Italy. His sermons were forceful, redolent of piety, full of solid instruction, abounding in apt citations from the Scriptures.

In the year 1251 or 1252 the master general of the order, by the advice of Albertus Magnus and Hugo a S. Charo (Hugh of St. Cher), sent Thomas to fill the office of Bachelor (sub-regent) in the Dominican studium at Paris. This appointment may be regarded as the beginning of his public career, for his teaching soon attracted the attention both of the professors and of the students. His duties consisted principally in explaining the "Sentences" of Peter Lombard, and his commentaries on that text-book of theology furnished the materials and, in great part, the plan for his chief work, the "Summa theologica".

In due time he was ordered to prepare himself to obtain the degree of Doctor in Theology from the University of Paris, but the conferring of the degree was postponed, owing to a dispute between the university and the friars. The conflict, originally a dispute between the university and the civic authorities, arose from the slaying of one of the students and the wounding of three others by the city guard. The university, jealous of its autonomy, demanded satisfaction, which was refused. The doctors closed their schools, solemnly swore that they would not reopen them until their demands were granted, and decreed that in future no one should be admitted to the degree of Doctor unless he would take an oath to follow the same line of conduct under similar circumstances. The Dominicans and Franciscans, who had continued to teach in their schools, refused to take the prescribed oath, and from this there arose a bitter conflict which was at its height when St. Thomas and St. Bonaventure were ready to be presented for their degrees. William of St-Amour extended the dispute beyond the original question, violently attacked the friars, of whom he was evidently jealous, and denied their right to occupy chairs in the university. Against his book, "De periculis novissimorum temporum" (The Perils of the Last Times), St. Thomas wrote a treatise "Contra impugnantes religionem", an apology for the religious orders (Touron, op. cit., II, cc. vii sqq.). The book of William of St-Amour was condemned by Alexander IV at Anagni, 5 October, 1256, and the pope gave orders that the mendicant friars should be admitted to the doctorate.

About this time St. Thomas also combated a dangerous book, "The Eternal Gospel" (Touron, op. cit., II, cxii). The university authorities did not obey immediately; the influence of St. Louis IX and eleven papal Briefs were required before peace was firmly established, and St. Thomas was admitted to the degree of Doctor in Theology. The date of his promotion, as given by many biographers, was 23 October, 1257. His theme was "The Majesty of Christ". His text, "Thou waterest the hills from thy upper rooms: the earth shall be filled with the fruit of thy works" (Psalm 103:13), said to have been suggested by a heavenly visitor, seems to have been prophetic of his career. A tradition says that St. Bonaventure and St. Thomas received the doctorate on the same day, and that there was a contest of humility between the two friends as to which should be promoted first.

From this time St. Thomas's life may be summed up in a few words: praying, preaching, teaching, writing, journeying. Men were more anxious to hear him than they had been to hear Albert, whom St. Thomas surpassed in accuracy, lucidity, brevity, and power of exposition, if not in universality of knowledge. Paris claimed him as her own; the popes wished to have him near them; the studia of the order were eager to enjoy the benefit of his teaching; hence we find him successively at Anagni, Rome, Bologna, Orvieto, Viterbo, Perugia, in Paris again, and finally in Naples, always teaching and writing, living on earth with one passion, an ardent zeal for the explanation and defence of Christian truth. So devoted was he to his sacred task that with tears he begged to be excused from accepting the Archbishopric of Naples, to which he was appointed by Clement IV in 1265. Had this appointment been accepted, most probably the "Summa theologica" would not have been written.

Yielding to the requests of his brethren, he on several occasions took part in the deliberations of the general chapters of the order. One of these chapters was held in London in 1263. In another held at Valenciennes (1259) he collaborated with Albertus Magnus and Peter of Tarentasia (afterwards Pope Innocent V) in formulating a system of studies which is substantially preserved to this day in the studia generalia of the Dominican Order (cf. Douais, op. cit.).

It is not surprising to read in the biographies of St. Thomas that he was frequently abstracted and in ecstasy. Towards the end of his life the ecstasies became more frequent. On one occasion, at Naples in 1273, after he had completed his treatise on the Eucharist, three of the brethren saw him lifted in ecstasy, and they heard a voice proceeding from the crucifix on the altar, saying "Thou hast written well of me, Thomas; what reward wilt thou have?" Thomas replied, "None other than Thyself, Lord" (Prümmer, op. cit., p. 38). Similar declarations are said to have been made at Orvieto and at Paris.

On 6 December, 1273, he laid aside his pen and would write no more. That day he experienced an unusually long ecstasy during Mass; what was revealed to him we can only surmise from his reply to Father Reginald, who urged him to continue his writings: "I can do no more. Such secrets have been revealed to me that all I have written now appears to be of little value" (modica, Prümmer, op. cit., p. 43). The "Summa theologica" had been completed only as far as the ninetieth question of the third part (De partibus poenitentiae).

Thomas began his immediate preparation for death.

Gregory X, having convoked a general council, to open at Lyons on 1 May, 1274, invited St. Thomas and St. Bonaventure to take part in the deliberations, commanding the former to bring to the council his treatise "Contra errores Graecorum" (Against the Errors of the Greeks). He tried to obey, setting out on foot in January, 1274, but strength failed him; he fell to the ground near Terracina, whence he was conducted to the Castle of Maienza, the home of his niece the Countess Francesca Ceccano. The Cistercian monks of Fossa Nuova pressed him to accept their hospitality, and he was conveyed to their monastery, on entering which he whispered to his companion: "This is my rest for ever and ever: here will I dwell, for I have chosen it" (Psalm 131:14). When Father Reginald urged him to remain at the castle, the saint replied: "If the Lord wishes to take me away, it is better that I be found in a religious house than in the dwelling of a lay person." The Cistercians were so kind and attentive that Thomas's humility was alarmed. "Whence comes this honour", he exclaimed, "that servants of God should carry wood for my fire!" At the urgent request of the monks he dictated a brief commentary on the Canticle of Canticles.

The end was near; extreme unction was administered. When the Sacred Viaticum was brought into the room he pronounced the following act of faith:

If in this world there be any knowledge of this sacrament stronger than that of faith, I wish now to use it in affirming that I firmly believe and know as certain that Jesus Christ, True God and True Man, Son of God and Son of the Virgin Mary, is in this Sacrament . . . I receive Thee, the price of my redemption, for Whose love I have watched, studied, and laboured. Thee have I preached; Thee have I taught. Never have I said anything against Thee: if anything was not well said, that is to be attributed to my ignorance. Neither do I wish to be obstinate in my opinions, but if I have written anything erroneous concerning this sacrament or other matters, I submit all to the judgment and correction of the Holy Roman Church, in whose obedience I now pass from this life.

He died on 7 March, 1274. Numerous miracles

attested his sanctity, and he was canonized by John XXII, 18 July, 1323. The monks of Fossa Nuova were anxious to keep his sacred remains, but by order of Urban V the body was given to his Dominican brethren, and was solemnly translated to the Dominican church at Toulouse, 28 January, 1369. A magnificent shrine erected in 1628 was destroyed during the French Revolution, and the body was removed to the Church of St. Sernin, where it now reposes in a sarcophagus of gold and silver, which was solemnly blessed by Cardinal Desprez on 24 July, 1878. The chief bone of his left arm is preserved in the cathedral of Naples. The right arm, bestowed on the University of Paris, and originally kept in the St. Thomas's Chapel of the Dominican church, is now preserved in the Dominican Church of S. Maria Sopra Minerva in Rome, whither it was transferred during the French Revolution.

A description of the saint as he appeared in life is given by Calo (Prümmer, op. cit., p. 401), who says that his features corresponded with the greatness of his soul. He was of lofty stature and of heavy build, but straight and well proportioned. His complexion was "like the colour of new wheat": his head was large and well shaped, and he was slightly bald. All portraits represent him as noble, meditative, gentle yet strong. St. Pius V proclaimed St. Thomas a Doctor of the Universal Church in the year 1567. In the Encyclical "Aeterni Patris", of 4 August, 1879, on the restoration of Christian philosophy, Leo XIII declared him "the prince and master of all Scholastic doctors". The same illustrious pontiff, by a Brief dated 4 August, 1880, designated him patron of all Catholic universities, academies, colleges, and schools throughout the world.

SOURCES

THE SUMMA
Thomas Aquinas. Summa theologiae. 2nd ed. Trans.Fathers of the English Dominican Province. At New Advent, www.newadvent.org.

BEER DESCRIPTIONS:
Descriptions for beers contained in this book were taken and modified from www.thebeerstore.ca

LIFE OF ST. THOMAS
Kennedy, Daniel. "St. Thomas Aquinas." The Catholic Encyclopedia. Vol. 14. New York: Robert Appleton Company, 1912. 11 Jul. 2016<http://www.newadvent.org/cathen/14663b.htm>.

Podcast

You should subscribe to Matt Fradd's new podcast, Pints With Aquinas. Every episode revolves around a question St. Thomas Answers in the Summa.

You can subscribe to the podcast at www.pintswithaquinas.com

Here are some reviews of the podcast:

"Matt Fradd might be my favorite Catholic/Christian apologist. He breaks down very complicated concepts into simpler terms and unpacks some deep philosophical questions with evidence and perspective. I look forward to hearing this podcast each week."

- DARREN, ITUNES REVIEW.

"Matt provides keen insights from [the] Summa Theologica, applies them to today's context, and presents them in a way that is both educational and fun, simply put, it's my new favorite podcast."

- MARRSEAN, ITUNES REVIEW

"This podcast has turned Aquinas from that distant, super-smart professor that doesn't want to talk to you into that friendly friar that you want to have a pint with."

- IVANROGAS, ITUNES REVIEW

"Matt Fradd's understanding of the Catholic faith is so helpful in deepening my faith and others. If you'd like to learn more about your faith, I highly suggest giving this a listen. Five stars all the way."

"This is a very professional sounding podcast and Matt Fradd's enthusiasm for the fatih is infectious. He does not shy away from hot or sensitive topics and sticks to what the Church teaches through the lens of the Angelic Doctor. When I recently became aware of this podcast I went back and listened to the archives. Just excellent."

Made in the USA
Lexington, KY
19 November 2016